act normal

THE HUGH MACLENNAN POETRY SERIES

Editors: Allan Hepburn and Carolyn Smart

Recent titles in the series

rushes from the river disappointment stephanie roberts
A House in Memory David Helwig
Side Effects May Include Strangers Dominik Parisien
Check Sarah Tolmie
The Milk of Amnesia Danielle Janess
Field Guide to the Lost Flower of Crete Eleonore Schönmaier
Unbound Gabrielle McIntire
Ripping down half the trees Evan J
whereabouts Edward Carson
The Tantramar Re-Vision Kevin Irie
Earth Words: Conversing with Three Sages John Reibetanz
Vlarf Jason Camlot
Unbecoming Neil Surkan
Bitter in the Belly John Emil Vincent
unfinishing Brian Henderson
Nuclear Family Jean Van Loon
Full Moon of Afraid and Craving Melanie Power
Rags of Night in Our Mouths Margo Wheaton
watching for life David Zieroth
Orchid Heart Elegies Zoë Landale
The House You Were Born In Tanya Standish McIntyre
The Decline and Fall of the Chatty Empire John Emil Vincent
New Songs for Orpheus John Reibetanz
the swailing Patrick James Errington
movingparts Edward Carson
Murmuration: Marianne's Book John Baglow
Take the Compass Maureen Hynes
act normal nancy viva davis halifax

act normal

nancy viva davis halifax

McGill-Queen's University Press
Montreal & Kingston • London • Chicago

ISBN 978-0-2280-1871-1 (paper)
ISBN 978-0-2280-1947-3 (ePDF)
ISBN 978-0-2280-1948-0 (ePUB)

Legal deposit fourth quarter 2023
Bibliothèque nationale du Québec

Printed in Canada on acid-free paper that is 100% ancient forest free (100% post-consumer recycled), processed chlorine free

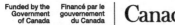

Funded by the Government of Canada | Financé par le gouvernement du Canada | Canada | Conseil des arts du Canada | Canada Council for the Arts

We acknowledge the support of the Canada Council for the Arts.

Nous remercions le Conseil des arts du Canada de son soutien.

McGill-Queen's University Press in Montreal is on land which long served as a site of meeting and exchange amongst Indigenous Peoples, including the Haudenosaunee and Anishinabeg nations. In Kingston it is situated on the territory of the Haudenosaunee and Anishinaabek. We acknowledge and thank the diverse Indigenous Peoples whose footsteps have marked these territories on which peoples of the world now gather.

Library and Archives Canada Cataloguing in Publication

Title: Act normal / Nancy Viva Davis Halifax.

Names: Davis Halifax, Nancy Viva, 1956- author.

Series: Hugh MacLennan poetry series.

Description: Series statement: The Hugh MacLennan poetry series | Poems.

Identifiers: Canadiana (print) 20230438431 | Canadiana (ebook) 20230438490 | ISBN 9780228018711 (softcover) | ISBN 9780228019480 (ePUB) | ISBN 9780228019473 (ePDF)

Classification: LCC PS8607.A957 A78 2023 | DDC C811/.6—dc23

This book was typeset by Marquis Interscript in 9.5/13 Garamond.

CONTENTS

act normal

INTRODUCTION

once a person is deemed not human
then all sorts of violence becomes acceptable
Eli Clare, *Brilliant Imperfection,* 118

from its beginnin' *act normal* has chosen illegibility & wilful uncertainty as one of its strategies \ to evade the grasp of the normative \ as endured by those institutionalized by & through the concept of normalcy

act normal starts in an institution where children categorized & constructed as intellectually inferior are placed into custodial care \ opened in 1876 as the hospital for [redacted] & [redacted] it closed in 2009 as the huronia regional centre[1]

act normal opens with my response to two documents where i use overwritin' as a form of erasure \ in overwritin' the chosen text is turned against itself \ written until illegibility is fixed through accumulation \ the first document \ 1927 \ *buck vs bell* references a case from the us supreme court regardin' the sterilization of [redacted] \ the second is the \ 1928 \ *alberta sexual sterilization act* \ an act which made it possible for thousands institutionalized to be sterilized \ in 1972 \ over forty years later \ alberta repealed the act

my research & readin' has been slow \ materials are difficult \ those who are considered other than human have & continue to be abandoned from our shared futurity \ with the introduction of reproductive genetic testin', fetuses identified as chromosomally different (e.g., down syndrome) are frequently terminated \

i have read multiple contemporary & historical texts that support eugenics \ refuse compassion \ create difference as dangerous \ *act normal* emerges through these & other texts \ through conversations \ memoirs & encounters with people who have been institutionalized at hrc & other total institutions \ workin' toward compassion & difference & the desire that a future can be secured \ *act normal* draws upon remembered conversations & silences \ bein' alongside \ imaginin' & speakin' with those who have been absented from our social fabric \ usin' archival materials \ court cases \ legislation \ transcripts \ case histories \ legal challenges \ photographs \ administrative \ medical & educational archives & artefacts\ i imagine the justice yet to come \ the manuscript reminds me that we are \ because they are not

centrin' itself in bodies that are off-centre *act normal* crips & destabilizes categories of meanin' \ crip unsettles normative expectations & is an endurance \ to crip writin' is to practice a movement counter to the hegemony of normative arts practices \ crip writin' does not fret about incoherence \ incredibility \ or a lack of reason

disability is often referenced as the problem \ from my position as disabled \ queer & crip i have learned to understand disability as undecidability \ context matters \ crip bodies exceed categories & labels \ crip art arises from bodies that create their own norms \ norms as uncertain & even unsweetened difference \ poetry re-situates knowledge practices as fragmented \ gestural \ incomplete \ unpredictable & embodied \ dressed in pyjamas \ sparkly

the act of readin' \ welcomes you to imagine & invite forms of knowledge \ other than \ *act normal* strives to evoke lives lost to our shared present \ it contests normative claims that would separate bodies into categories & further into institutions \ where they would not only be lost \ made invisible \ but they would also be absented from the rights received by those designated human \ *act normal* is resonant with possibility \ welcomin' an "unforeseeable diversity of the world" includin' "unheard & unexpected forms of knowledge ..." (Mignolo)

1927

BUCK v. BELL, Superintendent of State Colony [redacted] and [redacted]

1

and the equal protection of the laws.

2

by which the act protects the patients from possible abuse.

due process at law.

Cas. 765. Three generations of imbeciles are enough.

5

[illegible]

6

[illegible]

7

[illegible]

Chapter 37. The Sexual Sterilization Act (Assented to March 21, 1928).

HIS MAJESTY, by and with the advice and consent of the Legislative Assembly of the Province of Alberta, enacts as follows:

1. This Act may be cited as "The Sexual Sterilization Act."

2. In this Act, unless the context otherwise requires,—(a) "Mental Hospital" shall mean a hospital within the meaning of The Mental Diseases Act; (b) "Minister" shall mean the Minister of Health.

3.(1) For the purposes of this Act, a Board is hereby created, which shall consist of the following four persons: Dr. E. Pope, Edmonton; Dr. E. G. Mason, Calgary; Dr. J. M. MacEachran, Edmonton; Mrs. Jean H. Field, Kinuso. (2) Two members of the Board shall be medical practitioners nominated by the Senate of the University of Alberta and the Council of the College of Physicians and Surgeons respectively, and two members shall be persons other than medical practitioners appointed by the Lieutenant Governor in Council.

4. When it is proposed to discharge any inmate of a Mental Hospital, the Medical Superintendent or other officer in charge thereof may cause such inmate to be examined by or in the presence of the Board.

5. If upon such examination, the Board is unanimously of opinion that the patient might safely be discharged if the danger of procreation with its attendant risk of multiplication of the evil by transmission of the disability to progeny were eliminated, the Board may direct in writing such surgical operation for sexual sterilization of the inmate as may be specified in the written direction and shall appoint some competent surgeon to perform the operation.

[illegible]

[illegible]

8. This Act shall have effect only insofar as the legislative authority of the Province extends.

DO NOT SAY THAT YOU DID NOT KNOW 1960[2]

"(…) you have been told"

: Pierre Berton \ 6 January \ 1960

WILLISTON 1971 : failure & inhumanity[3]

i've been asked to investigate
lack of precision[4]
you must know
that & as such
i'll seek & pry

until satisfied

infallible[5]

A BETTER CHANCE OF PREVAILIN'

welcome to Orillia population 31000 incorporated 1867 & later a solution yes an asylum 1876 the shores of Lake Simcoe established to alleviate no because fear public delicacy confined children corrected by the science of improving stock practices (...) judicious mating[6] songs draw long letters tongues dry speech neglected inferior morality stuck bloodied & torn a roof a mouth broken the less suitable bred for sport

THE GOVERNMENT KNEW : THEY DID NOTHING

i want you to do the numbers \ do them \ until they are correct & i've forgotten the years of neglect \ until we blossom & leaf \ you remain pinned \ regret \ absorbed \ strung out over corridors \ visited by the thought of fire \ of needles piercin' \ inescapable \ a tied life \ a gatherin' of mortality \ a numberin' of names \ a disappearance of waltzes \ a shame of shakin' \ a disdain of bellies \ do nothin' \ wait \ be broke \ be grief

ASYLUM

you awestruck iron red
brick buildin's
hundreds of acres
the lake held promises
summer camp bonfires
marshmallows swimmin'
run & run & run
across fields a garden
to pick not yet tied
to the wrong side of this place
your face tipped
toward the lake clouds
promises you forget wavin'
good-bye the suitcase
you arrive with the stairs
you walk your last view
replaced by pacin'
the delinquency
of loathin' you flinch
the doors divert visitors
you are dressed redressed
rehearsed restrained soiled
unsorted laundry sour'd
light dandelion yellow

35 MILLION $[7]

first you have to have the number
without which there is no division
there were reports written it is likely

you should read those in the last days
furniture was gathered alongside
silverware straitjackets mortuary blocks

band uniforms the creation of a strange
parade numbers are not so easy to divide
12 years or 2807 good nights to glimpse

a world to decide how to harvest
the difference between 144
& 220 was not that great she thought

it was 74 but really that difference is
felt at bed time when there is a need
for a bed & not just a floor or cupboard

if you are lucky you forget that the patients
may have been seven-year-old *tiny tots*
with clouded minds[8] everyone learns to scrub

the wooden floors the lake at the foot
of the hill comin' inside the curve
of the basement corridor undersea

scenes a whale beached nothin' spectacular
in the original sense of the word there is
no spectacle here

only Berton's clouded tots

3 KILOMETRES AWAY

her last breath teeters
      &
is   dispersed

coyote delicates at acute angles
limbs slack   skin lax
                             over bone
weight   lightened
as vehicles   splinter
                             fur to pelt

where i live wvc[9] mortality is high

there rural arterials feed
distant registries
man's hands write at the edge of

marsh where she rendered
with incarnadine throat
leaves   language

THE CONSTITUTION OF SUBJECTS

you are constituted & regulated as a threat
included as a cost in preventive medical services
you walk a path that used to be an architectural drawing
exempt from minimum wage provisions

included as a cost in preventive medical services
you lie in the grass & look up
exempt from minimum wage provisions
your blossomin' sequestered

you lie in the grass & remember birds
the most attractive of choices fumbles at the latch
your blossomin' made barren
they render the letters that pronounce you incurable

the most attractive of choices include obedience
designate   :   patient   :   the Ontario hospital school
rendered unreasonable pronounced incurable
you are a public responsibility a mark against the norm

taken into custody at the Ontario hospital school
the consequences advance the law of mental hygiene
you are hidden become a forgotten public responsibility
you forget to button your cardigan

consequences subject you to medical interventions
your mind a landscape of forgotten
things you refuse to button your cardigan
disorders syllables tether you

your mind a locked landscape a young tree
form the letters & pronounce incurable
disorders perch syllables separate you
the future of a history \ its wretched stink of prevention

forms the letters & pronounces incurable
you needs a tether to tell the truth
the truth of history \ its wretched stink of prevention
the history of an unspoiled present

they needs a tether to tell your truth
you who're constituted & regulated as a threat
shadow history \ an unspoiled present
a path \ an architectural drawin'

ACT NORMAL : A CHARM

i might never be no-one that shiny

the beauty of a sequin'd self

what was stitched into heaven's drop

descendin'
comprisin' a life
uncoiled threads

n o i m i g h t n e v e r

] so whisper : hope [

snip the slender~~s~~
spittin' words into maulin' klists

drape the meagre~~s~~
in ordinary sorrow

sow the gaunt'~~s~~ coarse cotton with gossamer
substitute sleepies for slow~~s~~

fringe the day wider : be unburied & clothed

slip in :

mirror neurons		starry eye of deer
an eloquence of names
cracked shells		tattered grey fruit

: act normal

BEAUTY AT A PROPER DISTANCE \ IN SONG[10]

what a small thought it takes is a small part of the thought Wittgenstein had & i can't remember how much of the treatise i read maybe i finished the biography by Ray – ? could be his first or last name but recommended by a woman maybe K who told me it was a great read & there is a small thought somewhere wishin' for all those passed years & the women who sat beside & with me lives taken with daughters & dogs & death & dinner i pluck a chin whisker so fine no one but me would ever notice 'cept my fingers would turn to it over the day til they tore it from its root Suzy Lake let her chin whiskers grow singin' a mouth bright with red lipstick & i count each of her whiskers mourn my pluckin' that small thought about bein' a woman how it is to live with children with sons with daughters with histories to be filled torn beauty full

LISTENIN' OVER A DISTANCE

the metal bucket retains an edge   marks a limit
her hollows clamour   for you
to give over   let nothin' in

she serves her archive of endurance   :
sometimes the crack of ice   meltin'
in a bath   crowds the sides
of unwrapped bodies
drippin'
sticky gold   sap
the inscribed   thumps of sounds
she takes a direct hit
vibrates

neglectin' the *how* of transmission
she listens   :   a body's grace stilled
thawed
poured

you bring your lips to her side   &
whisper   :   i never knew

LAKE SIMCOE

the tumble forward
hissin' like a radiator
abandoned to beachside cottages
the scent returnin'
on the highway
like nitrogen or a verse
a paragraph of chickens

fatty skins fused
lapses how
trees are literally part of you

as each wordflower
curls phrases scars
wee mouths closed

attention varies its push
refuses excess

THE LONELY LAWS] hmmmm [

another
i remember] hmmmm [another
time
before we were
taken when
we were apple red
think of that colour
relinquished to porridge
wan
& hate seeded over
four hundred acres
ruins
outside the Beatles sing
she loves you *yeah* *yeah* *yeah*
inside
collapsed wings
rottin'
six years outside
six & six & six years inside where

time's pale strip rips memory

yeah yeah yeah

yeah yeah yeah

before

& later : huronia

: mourned claims

disputed against a list

custodial care

segregation

not what they say what i've done

can't be bad

yeah yeah yeah yeah

NASTY

mutterin' a secret over a cuppa coffee
at a quarter-a-cup counter
coulda left it in my handbag
cause no-one was listenin'
which means no one
not even the waitress
she was pourin' for other folk when i was tellin'
though there was a big fat bluebottle who coulda heard
could've trouble
tellin'
if it never got past the fly paper
anyway i left it there
easy like chewin' gum & bein' done stickinit
under your chair
i drank two cups sittin' at
that window
listenin' to souls beat against the glass chest of
night
knowin' this place was infected &
i had left this thing
this thing to spark a fever & catch
somethin' up
watchin' people walk
thinkin' about their last cuppa
their eyes reflectin'
an unthreadin' of lips
a crackin' of bones

DO YOU KNOW WHY YOU'RE HERE

outside a red brick buildin' a bright
late summer day   people kept
cancelled   part of
re-development   inside a room
inside the buildin' are a dog & a woman
the dog leans   the woman's hands rest
beneath the dog's harness   people
try to find   remember before
they are called to enter the long &
narrow rooms where men sit by closed
windows & patient
chairs wait close to doors
when their turn is called
the woman & the dog slowly walk the hall
the man gestures   :   sit   :   introduces himself
the woman sits on the close-to-the-door
easywash brown plastic patient chair & the dog leans

"do you know why you're here?" he asks & the woman knows
the question is not alone or hers
she is not sure   her mother
a colour   she no longer
remembers
an answer
in a room   unbroken
by light
          curled into a restless ball
beside   the dog
left in a room   the woman

thinks   something
"my doctor referred me"
something   this man
could give her
a harness   compounds would   adhere
her neurons   pharmaceuticals
metabolized & excreted
unregulated

"do you know why you're here ?"
the dog rises
clambers across her knees
leans against her
heart   their chests rise & fall
"do you know why you're here?"

LITHICS

what she listened to was a dry mouth a dust mote a dream of winter
howlin' its disquiet
she listened to the eraser unmarkin' walls where pencils lettered the
unpunctuated the disregarded & guarded
she listened to the crumpled whimpers of missed suppers to
what bruised & was sold ice cold in bars & was swatted or
tattooed or kissed or grew into milkweed to eyelashes gilt with
sun the restraint of canvas & bawlin' clothes flung like broken
teeth grounds' white socks swollen belly of a beaver split open
she listened to what moved inland needed its nose wiped had a
genetic legacy that defied your chromosomal account sank
under the shoulder of earth grew into blades of grass with
stark unshaven patience

she listened to what falls the crumblin' wings of monarchs the wild
stories of the dead she undressed each sound on the sun-
thickened shore listenin' to bone & cartilage shiftin' the
sucklin' of frosted elfin moths on lupines she clung to agitated
others & rumbly zeroes button-sized whirligigs calculatin' the
degrees the shudder of earth barren like a surprise the gnawin'
woodland mouse the berries eaten by birds veils of barbed
wire the blossomin' geometry of flowers foul life her hands
foldin' & unfoldin' slag callouses *terra rosa* the south sun
breaches sinks sings

ESCAPE

i promises myself an exit :
them who watches flinch when i turns
: south or right
: or toward the damp heat of the laundries

i listens for the scent of wood burnin' clear cold air autumn
: i can't read
: the signs
the buildin's never quite
tell me
only lead me deeper
along corridors where light
pools
on floors are
the outlines of memories
child shaped
leavings
to scrub & clean
to find
found
runnin' breathless collapsed in a corner
worn
steps
where i watches them
position keys
here life turns on
the words of others the palette of their
limitations

i am given over officially named : child
an exception
to the natural order

] o p e n a d o o r [

UNSPEAKABLE : WORDS a \ b\ c

a

[redacted]

b

[redacted]

c

[redacted]

[redacted]

[redacted]

d

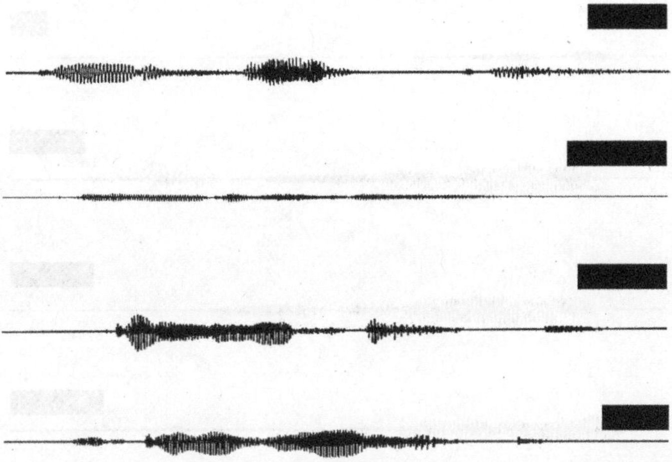

f

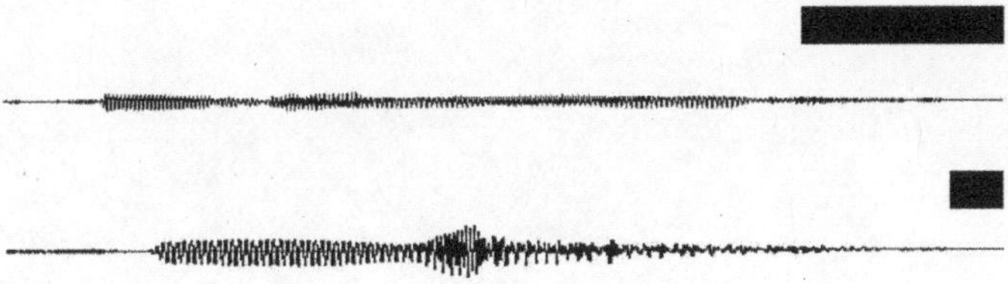

i

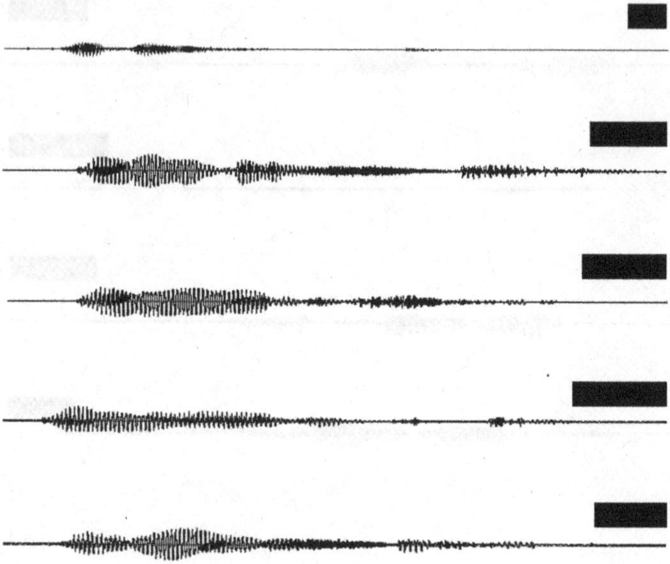

UNSPEAKABLE : WORDS j \ l \ m

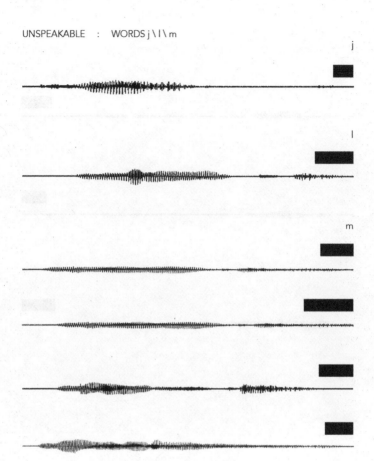

j

[redacted]

l

[redacted]

m

[redacted]

[redacted]

[redacted]

[redacted]

p

[redacted]

r

[redacted]

s

[redacted]

& WHAT IF YOU CANNOT

caress her back   there in the middle
you know the place she likes   :   her tell
the leanin'

& what if she is not faithful to the sounds given
what if she's an unanticipated copy
what if you cannot name what she has become

f e c u n d d e g e n e r a t e

& what if they take her apart & don't know
how to re-assemble her
pieces her intently undoneness   her moon phases

& what if you cannot find her
perch   the place where she can lurk   be
wretched   be   departed

m o r o n j o k e

& what if the arrival of desperation
becomes   :   the dirt under the tongue
of that thing we pretends is memory

b u r d e n m e n a c e

& what if   we cannot stop
                    cryin' if we
          truly   abjured   gutted

                    if we remembers

                                        we needs that caress

RAVEN 1952

we lie quietly
on a grassy bed
i've stopped cryin'
pine needles

brown from sun
relinquish their scent
a field ant scuttles
across stone it's always

like this   you lie
in the direction of
the sunken the planted
the emptied   your beak

directs me to sun's apex
bones tidily   slipped   & i wonder
about gravity
why the foot of a leaf   rests

in the hollow of your throat
& how wrong i am
when i read the black line
        of your wing
                                    as that which is yet to come

IF YOU WANT TO KNOW MORE

: remember the kettle
vultures boilin' over the bluffs

at dusk flared nostrils
: remember the fox wearin' a sweater

knit by herring gulls on a far island
: remember the red bald head

sunk deep she knows us
for the standin' tombs we are redraws

the illustrations of our end
her splendid visage freckled with blood

UNCALCULABLE

how many lost
  now rise alongside?
      ] grounds maintained
        by moderate lads [

& do i've enough
    toes & fingers & threads
        for that count?

  ] mild boys lead Galloway cows from fields to barns
        for milkin' [

those that were buried
  the winter
    heaves them up

] the severe trip nose-to-nose with earth kissin' bein' kissed [

i unravel the sheets use my toes to count off eleven
  knot ten threads
for seven days called week   check one of the boxes

- ■ mild
- ■ moderate
- ■ severe

not yet corpse worthy
  my aim is earth & worm
    a friendlier realm where

thin mud offers a damp shawl
along this road

i sink under
here
here
here

SOME KIND OF ASTRONAUT

still   out of sorts
the lack of a centre   this reelin'
never landin'   the world whirrs past   you
barely hangin' on to   the wish for an arm

you were supposed to be carried
to have someone
not tossed into the
carcass of night
the spinnin'
tearin' back thoughts that others had given

there is an unravellin'
around you not everything has become a
something
that is wrong
with you   a something that needs fixing
think hard   can you remember
what sinks
that word   :   okreinse   they ask

did you mean   :   aukernse
no nor teabag nor tree branch heavy with snow
the   words   birds flyin' past leaving trails of shite white
smears on white pages
& then   a bus
tightly packed   you have no weight
you are held   driven over arrows painted on roads

& the sinkin'   the thought that when you were small
they said they would protect you
hold you
lest mind follow a decayin' scent
& drag you to sinkin'
& whirrin'

PREVENTION & CORRECTION

Radford : writes our institutions might be understood
against
the weight of mornin'
of hands rememberin'
fences locks bars
as solutions
& maybe that is unfair

writes : sequestered
maybe our understandings are confined by authority
& our hands tied by what is
desired : a distance to isolate
& house
fear

a distance to part afflicted from hale
a distance written as an
absence of

children
written : deviant holy pitiable
dreaded

a distance
written to fund monumental public projects

] onebathtubfor144 [

death clothed : remains innocent
the years taken
unlit & narrowed

sequestered
the rationale : fear

change the shape of your shadow
retaliate
when they
turn to
look back you've vanished

RADFORD WRITES :

broken language \ walkway strip curtains creosote fragments \ the clarity of science \ childhood surrendered \ technical legislation surveilled casino rama stephen leacock \ sterile background to a foreground \ no more alert to wildness \ lake couchiching \ a garden \ the silence of light \ against the drone of inspection \ the buzzin' smear of blue bottles \ a startled & broken divination \ locked into a hard-to-reach place \ mnjikaning fish weirs \ delivered to science \ to follow authority \ a reliable genetic construction \ miserable hatchling \ held \ without comfort

THEIR FEAR INTENDS A FUTURE BARREN OF

you
phone & leave
such kind messages i listen capture you in the strokes
of letters
i don't know what to say
how to respond
to do small talk
our conversation is a way
to endure a future all of what has been refused

the shape of a phone is an instruction a gesture toward
conversation congregation of what cannot be
the falter of a soft slur the decomposition of hesitation
low frequency sounds of dread the sweat of a future buried

we are an oddly directed poem our large shaped circlin' &
togetherin' our awkward phrasin' the way we sing
dirt into stone rewritin' the brilliance of sun
our quakin' message : love : a guinea pig fed on greens
& oranges
your confidence
your out spoken queerness

APOLOGY (UNDER ERASURE) [11]

Mr **~~S~~peak**er. A government's responsibility is to **care** for its
people, to make sure they are **protect**ed and **safe**. And therein lies
a basic **trust** between **the state** and **the people**.
It is on that foundation of **trust** that **everything** else is built: **our**
sense of self, **our sense** of community, **our sense** of purpose. And
when that **trust** is **broken** with any one of us, we all lose
something – we are **all** diminished. I want to address a **matter** of
~~**trust**~~ before this house and my assembled colleagues, but I am
truly speaking to a group of people who have joined us this
afternoon and to the many others who could not be here
today. I am **humble**d to **welcome** to the legislature today former
residents of the Huronia Regional Centre and Rideau Regional
Centre in Smiths Falls and to also address former residents of the
Southwestern Regional Centre near Chatham, along with their
families and supporters. I want to **welcome** all of you and I want
to **honour** your determination and your **courage** and to **thank**
you for being here to bear **witness** to this occasion. Today, Mr
~~S~~peaker, we take **responsibility** for the **suffer**ing of these people
and their families.
I offer an **apology** to the men, women, and children of **~~O~~ntario**
who were **failed** by a model of institutional **care** for people with
developmental disabilities. We must **look** in the **eyes** of those
who have been affected, and to those they leave **behind**, and say:
"We are **sorry**." As Premier, and on behalf of all the people of
~~O~~ntario, I am **sorry** for your **pain**, for your **loss**es, and for the
impact that these experiences must have had on your **faith** in this
province, and in your government. I am **sorry** for what you and
your loved ones experienced, and for the **pain** that you **carry** to
this day. In the case of Huronia, some residents **suffer**ed **neglect**

and **abuse** within the very system that was meant to provide them
care. We **broke** faith with them – with you – and by doing so, we
diminished ourselves**.** Over a period of **generations,** and under
various governments, too many of these men, women, children,
and their families were deeply **harm**ed and continue to bear the
scars and the **consequence**s of this time. Their **humanity** was
undermined; they were separated from their families and **robbed**
of their potential, their **comfort**, their **safety,** and their **dignity**.
At Huronia, some of these residents were forcibly **restrained, left**
in **unbearable** seclusion**, exploited** for their **labour,** and **crowded**
into **unsanitary** conditions. And while the model of **care** carried
out by this institution is now acknowledged to have been deeply
flawed, there were also cases of unchecked physical and
emotional **abuse** by some staff and residents. Huronia was **closed**
in 2009 when **Ontario close**d the doors to its last remaining
provincial institutions for people with developmental disabilities.
Today, Mr Speaker, **we** no longer see people with developmental
disabilities as something "**other**." They are boys and girls, men
and women, with hopes and dreams like everyone else. In
Ontario, all individuals **deserve** our support, our respect and our
care. We must **look** out for one another, take **care** of one another;
challenge ourselves to be led by our sense of moral purpose
before all else. Today, we strive to support **people** with
developmental disabilities so they can live as independently as
possible and **be more** fully included in all aspects of their
community. As a society, we seek to **learn** from the **mistakes** of
the past. And that process **continue**s. I **know**, Mr Speaker, that
we have **more** to do. And so we will protect the **memory** of all
those who have **suffer**ed, **help** tell their stories, and ensure that
the lessons of this time are not **lost**. We are so **sorry**. Thank **you**.

THE GRAVITY OF CARROTS

each memory is lit by its own small moon
Don McKay, *Another Gravity*, 62

i had not thought about carrots til
you asked me to kneel & dig
scatter seed

you lived loss
large babies   bodies
wintered over
til a shovel could gain purchase in the soil

you lived in a house off the highway
near the penitentiary   a double glider swing
chickens & a bitch called Tiny
flat white coat black & brown patches

you taught your daughters to kneel
to scramble down the cliffs to the *baie*
the salt water buoyin' their soiled

bodies   rain & fog
swimmin' alongside
they stripped   clothes scattered

you watch   :   a lifetime of diggin'
& raisin' & buryin'   :   hold your breath
as they dive

under rooted floral parasols

RCT[12]

there are measures we are given \ measures made as we calculate \ falterin' protective measures that prove \ there are measures used by industry \ by schools by publics \ they are held like flags \ there are measures for the distortion of integrity \ that sleep & flag \ there are animals broken \ by delicate proofs \ that measure the risk & the costs for publics \ for incarcerated adolescents \ white markets \ there are tests that measure the minimally protected \ effectively toxic \ without benefit \ as accomplishments of equations \ there are measures that risk \ the shattered \ the harmed \ the cured \ the exploited the adversely wise \ the seriously adequate \ the broken in pieces \ there are lines written \ without measure \ there are measures protected by lines given \ distorted by reports of delicate sounds \ there are lines without measure \ there is writin' of exquisite shape \ there are hearts & lungs given \ there are numbers \ that pulse

WHAT IS LEFT

what is left in these rooms
    is a staff smock curtain rubber stamp wooden mallet square nail   prize winnin' cheese an organ scale a grind stone the will of an other
what is left in these rooms
    is what is made from cloth an adoration of numbers is a count of storybooks with animals with clothes is the way a child smells like crayons an exchange for a name an exchange for a wage
what is left
    is placed in boxes is a baby doll becomes evidence a breakin' order a lack of scrutiny
what is left
    is what could let me imagine the tender of care is what turns me toward theft what is left knows the damage done by thinkin' rock instead of paper an upheaval of earth
what is left in these rooms
    is what is not given extraordinary measures exhaustion
what is left is
    breakfast a peach an onion shirts & trousers is what convinces is a concern a lack a scrutiny the inability to persuade the subject of an inquiry paper patterns a sequence of tests

what remained

was a kind of place without song or birds exiled from
all thought shadows & their obedience the unspoken
what divides a thing on your tongue the despair of a
safe category the slope of a hill a name language that
refuses that angle

THE LIGHTING OF THE WARDS

call the buildin's
cottages & you feel the sun on your skin the impossibility
of blackflies torn jammies
a nest of homely comfort wrapped in a throw you
grasp the worn edges of summer
barometric pressure
fallin' headaches
when you are sortin' laundry
something about bein' broken

the light these moments

& you

forget

call the buildin's
cottages nestle them along a lake
unmute the call of loons enter potato sack races
peach pie & hotdog eatin' contests
you are all first-prize winners you have survived
your old feelings
tell yourself stories about
what to remember what it looks
like love measure the reflection of light
the decay of a shufflin' walk
the weary
sounds

gestures direct
you
there

call the buildin's
cottages the domain of the mundane of spoons
soup n crackers
toasted marshmallows
display the children
use ordinary lights natural if possible
stand them against a newly painted wall
warm white with a hint of ochre
be wary of reds
of deepenin' shadows
haul the stones
from graveyard to backyard to grave
plant them above
where you lie
nose pressed
skyward
ask : what light

TO FAIL MORE FULLY

i was peachin'
boisterous unburied & clothed
awake in my nest
drawin'
days where the size of the wolf
doesn't
matter
wolf protects me : a huggin'
animal
kissin'
brittle bodies of the dead potato bugs
savourin' old women who in forgettin'
vertical demands
lie on their backs
glasses : hearin' aids discarded laughin'

wolf flirts finds a semi-detached
wary sanctuary

i measure what is between us
against the curve
we are
stammerin' at the speed of

persuasion

can a sentence bear the weight \ of a beautiful tongue \ suffer through a war \ language doesn't have\ answers but as soon as i closes \ my eyes stories ring in oats & cranberries \ my mornin' porridge strawberries \ raspberries fourth floor \ walk-ups

: these are dreams :

a man walks north followin' \ the scent of a heart \ another man walks a white & black – papillon cross[13] \ there are two \ when my world collapses \ one being me the other an other me \ the first attends upon the ghosts of our sleep \ the other weeds the shape of our desperate intention \ our altitude & distance

] THAT THE AFTER ME IS UNCERTAIN IS CERTAIN [14

the work of evenin' screams
you are just slightly ahead of your past
pacin' toward a moment of clarity

a gatherin'
an anxiety of tellin's
words sutured to spines

proofs to arguments
on one page
a man is angry

a woman sings
& on that one : her ears
close like flowers

keep goin' read the one holdin' the string
read how her balloon catches how she rises
moves toward cotton
candy waves to the shaky
left-behinds there'll soon be none

by 2050 the books of memory
will've been picked clean
what points to you now past erased
ripped

A DISTANCE TO EASE THE LONELY

close your eyes
describe what you see
tell me :

it's early
& cold some children still
sleep hunger with open eyes

there's a noise
& you're on the shore &
you feels the heat before the fire is lit
the ache of the shovel before diggin'

but you've no memory can't remember what
eclipses the present
all you knows : the kitchen's gone silverware's locked
away
the moons are fallin'

& you falls in their wake
you're not what's expected
the door's been made : it opens & closes
: finds
a child : the colour of grief

THE WRITIN' OF HAPPY BEGINS : WHAT I CAN & CANNOT

i wants to write \ & like you \ i waits patiently \ for those who were & are \ the happys \ rockin' & fidgetin' \ the joys \ in unkempt clothes \ the wonders \ impossibly kind \the scent of polish \ of keys in locks \ helps me assemble \ the unwept & the halfway to dead \ i takes what the discards \ offer \ mouth to sky \ we eats \ the leaves of hunger's feast \under rooms that gather us \ the sounds of short waves \ a frequency \ an architecture of morality \ spells us \ we becomes that thing \ what you don't remember\ can not be forgotten \

i wants you to imagine \ the cast of light \ no where left \ to fall \ your affliction \ our soles fingered with earth \

THE BUILDIN'S NOT THE CURE

when the light dies
a door is locked   & the peril of you
stands   at the front of a room
your face swollen   with your refusal

what wriggles out
is what
you learn to hide

policy's calculation of optimum distances
exposes muscles   of responsibility

sliced into a bowl
the spaces between   lies
gaps in the chains of twelve-foot fences
the signs   warning

you wonder   was it really like that
unsure if you is the one in the green sweater
walkin' up granite steps   being stripped
the heavens   the colour of leftovers   the offerin's
small carcasses   surrendered   your past
sequestered   miles from home   years
the heavens bumped & warped

under the wolf moon a solitary wasp
    clambers through salted lands
your skin fire   your mouth light

MATTERS OF CARE :

] werepeatwhatwehavebeentaught [

friday first dustin' of snow
the guy from the convenience store's out
cigarette danglin' shovellin' head down
smoke risin' & a dog at full speed
barrellin' & beamin'
forever

] myheartwantstheseechoes [

wants to be a word wants to warn
to break to know
the how to reflected in the puddle
framed by dirt & sky

] makefasttohappy [

ring me
we'll talk
we'll look at the figures
the costs of splittin' us from the human

] immigrantpaupercriminalfeebleminded [

YOU ARE JUST
]   for those who were & are   [

it is possible that we are not human beings to them
Leonel, in Carolyn Forché, *What You Have Heard Is True,* 313

] notwhatwethoughtyouwouldbe [

she says   let's order pizza
soft drinks   & cookies
          a feast's   best
when you're surrounded
by tremblin' walls
     & walkin' along corridors
     where rooms gather   ghosts   march
     there'll be singin'
               & polyester
they'll be there
          they'll be there
                         with their grammars

]   underdirectcusodialcarebythegovernment   [

she says   that's ok
shows you how   to curl into yourself

says   :   you're the flower
               you're what is

let them ask their questions
let them think they're safe

] overcrowdedisolatedundermaintained [

they've gathered & sorted
us matched & marched
us dressed in small stones & sand
they wakes us
to bodies not of our choosin'

] threegenerationsenough [

says don't forget to shine
as they lines you up

for boiled dinner
never yawn
never give an openin'

remember utility knife duct tape
string chicken wire
somethin'

CONSENT TO INVESTIGATION TREATMENT OR OPERATIVE PROCEDURE

the institution's not a metaphor \ & the child's not a creation of metaphor \ trained \ yes \ by the ringin' of a bell \ for silence \ to queue \ to piss \ to walk \ to eat \ to shit \ to sleep \ at first light \the child \ sighs

] listen [

to who they wants to be \ an echo \ unafraid of the dark \ still too small to reach the switch \ someone's turnin' \ lights off & off \ & you remember your fear of the dark \ drawn as a line \ an exact point of origin & end \ chapped & cracked \ red & raw \

] listen [

was there ever \ a kind lie \ was there ever \ only & always hard shit \ broken teeth \ grim against flesh \ a blighted land \ memory \ held behind glass \ dissolves & blossoms \ a doll \ naked on the mattress of a crib cage \ hair in desperate need of brushin' \ & at last light \

] listen [

the clouds chant

lovelovelove

lovelove love

love

love

love

love

love

love

A THREAT HAD TO EXIST IN ORDER TO EXPAND & SUSTAIN THE INSTITUTION[15]

not so long ago a boy filled with the sun's shine
chummed around   played
getting' into trouble
games   discovered birthday cake
a way to pal around with girls
where do bad boys go
but what does any of that matter   when
a boy is named   :   menace   :   burden
        & finds that he's been delivered
                like dinner   to a place
                where a boy's heart pounds &
                                home is disappeared

where do bad boys go

the boy is tryin'
the boy yearns
toward waves   reads
the shore   wishes in his heart to be
        fish

h o m e

THERE IS] must be [EVIDENCE : AN "INQUIRY INTO THE ADEQUACY OF CARE" 1848[16]

you were under their protection
two or three means
how many buried
facts
movin' targets
numbers won't hold
whether anything can be done
there's birth
there's refusin'
there is loss never
administered gently
they ask for proof
of harm *six homes* *six months*
should be enough

lovely skin
simply impossible

THE WEIGHT OF DISREGARD

2:15 am

dream moves
traverses sinew & bone asks
can you count
can you read

mutters : i was once a small thing
disruptive wearin' a shirt
letters faded
& crazed by the tumble of a dryer

4 am

under dark of moon
remembers
& growls : it's time

puts on her face & feet
head down follows
the stench of indifference

5:36 am

everyone dreams these are our moments
half-way through
darkness sink
tread water

10:19 am

close eyed   fragments   gather
    map   blue lines   blue   muscle
        the sparrow   the scent

A COMPLETE SEVERIN'

you break when you can't
return when your bones
sink when you are
one without
life

revised by earth & world
you are the edge of human
their mistake shuffled
til you are not

world rewrites as easily as she forgets
you walkin' on her
are given the shape of hands
mittens always two or three remember
sheep broken

bones missin' teeth
a spell for mendin' life
being milkweed
breakin' tarmac

REDACTED : STIGMATA OF [redacted]

The unrecognized [redacted] *is the most dangerous element in the community.*
From a biological stamp the [redacted] *is an inferior human being.*[17]

death & life   institutions follow policy & procedures
sixteen bunks   the bottom ones   for two
      later more   policy insists you open your mouth
      speak what they have placed there

institutionalize all [redacted] *of reproductive age to prevent their*
breeding and, if necessary, *sterilize them.*[18]

so much openin'

your tongue sticks

lips burn

blood is the lubricant &   *if necessary*
becomes *of course*

[redacted] *advocated the "the painless destruction of*
[redacted] & [redacted]" [19]

administration is never   gentle   walks you into a broken   branch
eye level
to the observer little happens   an object subjected to the
rhythms of the
institution   cleaves

subtractsdeletesvanishesdisappears

[redacted] *sole interest was research. His concern with*
the [redacted]

was not

with their training and welfare, but as he frankly put it "in getting them off the earth."[20]

whatisunwrittenisnotunforgotten

SYSTEMATIC ACTION OF A WILL UPON ANOTHER IN VIEW OF ITS IMPROVEMENT[21]

begin with good intentions
the improvement of humanity
the necessary edits
there's *no limit*[22]

begin with facts
the measurement of buildin's usin'
the height of a child
the history of water
the devout nature of burnin'

yourexperienceofsorrow

begin with knowin'
children are lookin'
at the way your mouth
tongue
teeth
prepare words

overwhelmingauthorityofknowledge

begin by relinquishin' fear

all feelin'

IN ITS STATEMENT OF DEFENCE, THE PROVINCE DENIED THAT ANY ABUSE OR MISTREATMENT HAPPENED AT THE INSTITUTION[23]

dooropenslightscigarette
takesalongdraglightsflicker

slow down watch
she blows out the match

how many years she wearin'
workin' the counter at the five & dime

hopin' 14 hours & 52 bucks
is a bus ticket

she serves them what comes
she's good with orders

only lately forgettin'
who had medium double doublecreamsweetener at closin'

she resets the booths \ checks stock backorders straws \
mustard \ meagre courtesy napkins being wrung

by flex of thought
sees herself : a gaudy wilt

her thoughts remaindered marked down
a rival to the average :

s t u b s c i g a r e t t e o u t d o o r c l o s e s

PROPERLY APPLIED STERILIZATION WILL BE OF GREAT BENEFIT TO HUMANITY[24]

you's marvellous \ unafraid of the dark \ the within \ of light \ is what slips you up \ it's when you pray for

s l a t e s i l t l i c o r i c e o n y x p e w t e r c o a l

& the day grows into its turnin' \ you're standin' at the top of a hill \ its serene long & shortness \ adults circlin' \ some had been children \ they'll tell you what you've been born to \ there's a word or not \ maybe

g u n m e t a l c a r b o n e a r t h s h a k e r

practice \ lifted from the French \ coupled with English \ carved from Latin \ drawn in the shape of a thread \ breath \ as it rises \ as it falls \ look to the sky puddle \ to muddy truths \ our day-by-day is for burnin' \ we're kindlin'

c h a r c o a l b o n e o b s i d i a n

SOMETHING YOUR MOTHER CROCHETED \ HELD NEXT TO SKIN \

workin' the early shift \ you bring \ home along
as you walk \ zipper undone
red tea towel across your shoulder
a word or two for the day \ scratched under skin

e n c h a n t m e n t e l e c t r o n

you've degreased & dried the words
marked the topography
of your fragile state \
your scrap of lace \

d o n o t t o u c h

a principle of life on the far side of radiant
magnifications of ordinary days \

& you see
you're the dark stain's
        dreamin' \
        you're evidence

b o t h a n d

c a n a d a m e a n i n g u n b e a r a b l e

NOTES

1 Huronia is a reference to the huronia regional centre \ its history of names includes the convalescent [redacted] asylum, 1861–70, which re-opened in 1877 as the Hospital for [redacted] and [redacted]. By 1885 it became the orillia asylum for [redacted] \ Ontario hospital school and finally the huronia regional centre which closed in 2009

2 Pierre Berton, "What's Wrong at Orillia: Out of Sight Out of Mind," *Toronto Daily Star*, 6 January 1960, reproduced in Berton, "Huronia"

3 Williston, *A Report*, 10

4 Ibid.

5 Ibid.

6 Galton, 1883, 17

7 $35 million was the sum that the government offered in settlement re the class action lawsuit. the settlement process was complex for many reasons \ this poem returns to the Berton article where he writes "tiny tots with clouded minds"

8 Berton, "What's wrong at Orillia," reproduced in Berton, "Huronia"

9 WVC : wildlife vehicle collisions

10 Lake, "Beauty at a Proper Distance/In Song"

11 On 9 December 2013 Premier Kathleen Wynne of Ontario delivered Ontario's "Apology to Former Residents of Regional Centres For People with Developmental Disabilities" at the provincial legislature. The apology was delivered a week after the Huronia Class Action Lawsuit was settled for $35 million.

12 RCT \ randomized controlled trial \ the gold standard of scientific knowledge

13 a papillon is a small & intelligent dog \ companion

14 thanks to PS for the title

15 Trent, *Inventing the Feeble Mind*, 238

16 Howe, *Report Made to the Legislature of Massachusetts upon Idiocy*, 1, in Trent, *Inventing the Feeble Mind*, 13

17 Trent, *Inventing the Feeble Mind*, 157

18 Ibid., 163
19 Ibid., 134
20 Ibid., 157
21 Burghardt, *Broken*, 17
22 Ibid.
23 Alamenciak, "Class-Action Settlement Amounts to 'Hush Money'"
24 Ibid.

SELECT BIBLIOGRAPHY

Alamenciak, Tim. "Class-Action Settlement Amounts to 'Hush Money,' Says Family of Huronia Survivor." *Remember Every Name*, 27 September 2013. https://www.remembereveryname.ca/class-action-settlement-amounts-to-hush-money-says-family-of-huronia-survivor.

Berton, Pierre. "Huronia: Pierre Berton Warned us 50 Years Ago." *Toronto Star*, 20 September 2013, originally published in 1960. https://www.thestar.com/news/insight/2013/09/20/huronia_pierre_berton_warned_us_50_years_ago.html.

Burghardt, Madeline C. *Broken: Institutions, Families, and the Construction of Intellectual Disability*. Montreal and Kingston: McGill-Queen's University Press, 2019.

Butler, Judith. *Precarious Life: The Powers of Mourning and Violence*. London and New York: Verso, 2006.

Clare, Eli. *Brilliant Imperfection*. Durham, NC: Duke University Press, 2017.

Forché, Carolyn. *What You Have Heard Is True: A Memoir of Witness and Resistance*. Penguin Books, 2020.

Galton, Francis. "Eugenics: Its Definition, Scope, and Aims." *American Journal of Sociology* 10, no. 1 (1904): 1–25.

– "Hereditary Talent and Character." *Macmillan's Magazine* 12 (1865): 157–66 and 318–27.

– *Inquiries into Human Faculty and its Development*. New York: Macmillan and Company, 1883.

Lake, Suzy. "Beauty at a Proper Distance/In Song." 2001–02, 2011. Self-portraits, digital chromogenic transparencies and light boxes. https://www.suzylake.ca/beauty-at-a-proper-distance#7.

McKay, Don. *Another Gravity*. Toronto: McClelland & Stewart, 2000.

Mignolo, Walter D. "Coloniality: the Darker Side of Modernity." In *Modernologies: Contemporary Artists Researching Modernity and Modernism*, edited by Sabine Breitwisser, 39–49. Catalogue of the Exhibit. Barcelona, Spain: Modernologia/Modernologies/Modernology at the Museum of Modern Art, 2009.

Province of Alberta. *An Act to Amend the Sexual Sterilization Act*. Statutes of the Province of Alberta. 1937. http://www.ourfutureourpast.ca/law/page.aspx?id=2968369.

Trent, James W., Jr. *Inventing the Feeble Mind: A History of Mental Retardation in the United States*. Vol. 6. Berkeley, Los Angeles, and London: University of California Press, 1994.

US Supreme Court. *BUCK v. BELL*. Superintendent of State Colony Epileptics and Feeble Minded, 1927. https://www.law.cornell.edu/supremecourt/text/274/200.

Van Wagenen, Bleeker. "Preliminary Report of the Committee of the Eugenic Section of the American Breeders' Association to Study and to Report on the Best Practical Means for Cutting Off the Defective Germ-Plasm in the Human Population." 1912, published online by Georgia State University College of Law, *Buck v Bell Documents*, 2009.

Williston, W. *A Report to The Honourable A.B.R. Lawrence, M.C., Q.C. Minister of Health on Present Arrangements for the Care and Supervision of Mentally Retarded Persons in Ontario*. Department of Health, Government of Ontario, August 1971.

WITH GRATITUDE

the poems are an embodied praxis \ resonant with material bodys in their fluid unfinished & exquisite becomings \ about institutions & the kinds of bodys that circulate within & in proximity to institutional walls \ the necessity of uncertainty \ gifted to the humans & the other- & more-than-humans who keep showin' up \ my teachers & mentors \ the inconvenients – my sister poets \ my sparkly wonderfuls Cynthia Merle Viva Karmah Jonah Stan Annie – kin comrades & family \ Cindy Fujimoto who listens to me within & beyond the brackets \ Sid for long walks & conversations about pain & illness \ being in & away from community\ for all of the unexpected meetings & collisions

York University for a research release & a sabbatical \ the Ontario Arts Council for a Literary Creation grant

appreciation & thanks to Carolyn Smart \ Joanne Pisano \ Alyssa Favreau \ Jacqueline Michelle Davis \ Filomena Falocco & the many others of MQUP

finally i thank the editors of the following journals for publishing the following poems \ some in their present & others in earlier forms

"Do Not Say that You Did Not Know 1960"; "A Better Chance of Prevailin'"; "35 Million $"; "The Constitution of Subjects": PUBLIC *66*: *Access Aesthetics*

"Consent to Investigation Treatment or Operative Procedure": *the way out is the way in: an anthology of disabled poets*, edited by Stuart Ian McKay. Toronto: League of Canadian Poets

"Listenin' over a Distance"; "Escape"; "What is Left": *La Presa* 9 (Spring 2020), poems translated by Juan Romero Vinueza

"The Lonely Laws] hmmmm [": *Hamilton Arts & Letters* 12, no. 2, Dis\ability Poetics: Imaginary Safe House

"Do You Know Why You're Here?": *Canadian Journal of Disability Studies* 8, no. 4, Survivals, Ruptures, Resiliences

"3 Kilometres Away": *Wordgathering: A Journal of Disability Poetry and Literature* 36

"Act Normal : A Charm"; "Uncalculable": *Room* 41, no. 4

"Apology (Under Erasure)": *Canadian Journal of Disability Studies* 6, no. 3 (2017), Institutional Survivorship